GET YOURSELF O

1.50

Forthcoming titles in this series will include

- *Winning Negotiation Tactics!*
- *Basic Business Finance!*
- *Successful Business Planning!*
- *Winning CVs!*
- *Getting Hired!*
- *Managing People for the First Time!*
- *Successful Interviewing Techniques!*
- *Letter Writing for Winners!*
- *Winning Telephone Techniques!*

Do you have ideas for subjects which could be included in this exciting and innovative series? Could your company benefit from close involvement with a forthcoming title?

Please write to David Grant Publishing Limited
80 Ridgeway, Pembury, Tunbridge Wells, Kent TN2 4EZ
with your ideas or suggestions.

Mike Levy

60 Minutes Success Skills Series

First published 1997 by
David Grant Publishing Limited
80 Ridgeway, Pembury, Kent TN2 4EZ United Kingdom

60 Minutes Success Skills Series is an imprint of
David Grant Publishing Limited

British Library Cataloguing in Publication Data
A CIP catalogue record for this book is available from the British Library

ISBN 1-901306-00-3

Cover design: Steve Haynes

Text design: Graham Rich

Production editor: Paul Stringer

Typeset in Futura by
Archetype, Stow-on-the-Wold
http://ourworld/compuserve.com/homepages/Archetype

Printed and bound in Great Britain by
T.J. International, Padstow, Cornwall

This book is printed on acid-free paper

CONTENTS

Welcome: About *Get Yourself Organised!* 7

Chapter 1: Clear desk, clear conscience **11**
Why you should have a clear desk
How to start clearing the mess
Simple but effective filing systems
Ten commandments for sorting out your desk life

Chapter 2: Make priorities, meet deadlines **19**
Stop being a fire-fighter
Meet "impossible" deadlines
Prioritise
Profit from lists and planners
Exploit your diary
Tactics for prioritising and meeting deadlines

Chapter 3: Delegate with confidence **29**
Delegate – or sink
What is delegation?
How to recognise what to delegate
Selling delegation to those around you
How much to delegate
Knowing who to delegate to
What's cramping your delegation style?
Tips for delegating effectively

Chapter 4: Procrastination, paper and phones **41**
Stop procrastinating
Tackle your paperwork
Keep your in-tray empty
Make the phone your friend
Master your paperwork and the phone, now!

Chapter 5: Make the most of meetings **51**
Meetings under the microscope
How to cut out wasteful meetings
How to evade meetings
Minimise the pain
All-important preparation

Take control
Making meetings effective

Chapter 6: Making computers work for you 57
What your computer can do for you
Managing your information
Office suites – the all-in-one solution
Organising your life the electronic way
The paperless office
Get the most from computers

WELCOME

ABOUT *GET YOURSELF ORGANISED!*

Can you learn how to banish chaos and transform yourself into a paragon of organisational virtue in just one hour? The answer, quite simply, is "YES".

The only bit of waffle in the book

The 60 Minutes Success Skills Series is written for people with neither the time nor the patience to trawl through acres of jargon and page-filling waffle. Like all of the books in the series, *Get Yourself Organised!* has been written in the belief that you can learn all you really need to know quickly and without fuss. The aim is to provide effective tips you can use straight away.

Is this book for you?

Get Yourself Organised! is packed full of useful and practical advice for the terminally disorganised. Do you recognise any of these symptoms?

- ***Disorganised desk and office – you never can seem to find that vital bit of paper.***
- ***Life is one long panic – everything seems to be "top priority". "Help – what do I do first?!"***
- ***You're incredibly overworked and stressed out – but you can't seem to find anybody trustworthy or capable to delegate the work to.***
- ***It's so much easier to put things off until tomorrow – you'll be in a better frame of mind then.***
- ***You seem to waste most of your life in an endless round of useless meetings and pick up extra work for your trouble.***
- ***You know that the computer sitting in the corner could help, but you're too scared to switch it on.***

If any of these strike a chord, this quick, no-bull guide is just what you need.

Kick your bad habits and make your work life calmer and more efficient.

- ***Use your desk as a tool, not a cluttered dumping ground.***
- ***Meet deadlines by prioritising your work properly.***
- ***Delegate the right work to the right people in the right way.***

- *Don't dither, do it now.*
- *Cut meetings down to size.*
- *Make the most of the technology at your disposal.*

How to use the book

The message in the 60 Minutes Success Skills Series is "it's OK to skim". Each book is written in a way that allows you to flick through and find the help you most need. *Get Yourself Organised!* is a collection of "hands on" tips that will help you become the organised person you've always wanted to be. You don't have to read it all at once or try to do everything advised straight away.

You will find that there are some graphic features used throughout the book:

These mean: "Something to think about" – they set the scene and identify the problems by prompting you to think about situations which will instantly feel familiar.

With the problem diagnosed, these features give you ideas for an action plan – they will help you to change your behaviour patterns in a positive way.

These features appear at the end of each chapter. They are checklists which summarise all of the advice given throughout the chapter. Similar features also appear within chapters which are overflowing with tips!

As you read through the book, you will come across lots of tips and practical advice on how to make more of your time by organising your work efficiently. You could start by just going straight to any of the boxed features, which will ask you either to think about a problem or to do something about it and give you some ideas. If you're really pushed for time, you can always go direct to the tips at the end of each chapter.

The chapter tip summaries are also a useful reminder of what's where when you come back to look at this book in the future.

Good luck.

Clear Desk, Clear Conscience

Chapter 1

What's in this chapter for you

Why you should have a clear desk
How to start clearing the mess
Simple but effective filing systems
Ten commandments for sorting out your desk life

Take two minutes to look at your desk. Are you proud of it? Is it a model of tidiness and good order? Or is it a hopeless clutter of papers, files, unwashed coffee mugs, and bent paperclips? Look at your in-tray (if you have one). Is it full of genuine things "to do" or, like many people, are you using it as just another place to dump papers?

Why should you have a clear desk?

> *"I get so overwhelmed with paperwork that I look for any available space to shove it – in- or out-trays, the top of the desktop printer, anywhere I can find. I've also got an impressive collection of old cardboard boxes bulging with unchecked documents."*
>
> **– Pam Flew, accounts administrator**

Does this sound familiar? Your desk is your primary workspace. It is, or should be, the engine of your working day, feeding you with relevant and timely activities – and helping you to get them done.

> **A desk should be nothing more than a clearing house of work in progress. It should not become a storage area. What do you see when you look at yours?**

It's easy to let your desk become a dumping ground instead of an invaluable tool to help you in your job. It can be a permanent and highly visual reminder of all the jobs you haven't done. It can also be a secret place where urgent work gets lost.

If you need some motivation to tidy your desk, consider the reasons why a disorganised and untidy desk is **bad** news.

An untidy desk is bad for your image

There are times when it is important what other people think about you – especially when "other people" include important clients, colleagues and the boss. No matter what the circumstances, an untidy desk can give the impression that you are a disorganised malingerer.

You think	Others think
It shows that I'm a radical	It shows that s/he's a lazy so and so
I've got better things to do	S/he couldn't care less
It proves I'm really overworked	It proves s/he's totally disorganised
I know where everything is	No wonder s/he never keeps deadlines

An untidy desk is bad for your work

Messy desks breed lost papers, documents and files. Lost or delayed work means lost time and maybe even lost customers. A vast amount of time can be wasted hunting for buried paperwork.

An untidy desk is bad for your health

Dealing with ever-growing mountains of paperwork can lead to increased stress levels and panic attacks. Managing your desk is a vital way of making your workload more manageable.

Still not convinced? Maybe you're one of those who still believes in the hoary old chestnut, "tidy desk, sick mind" (probably written by a highly efficient and well-organised business guru). OK, maybe putting it in financial terms will convince you to do something about that desk:

- ❑ ***The average person can waste up to one whole day per month in searching for missing papers.***
- ❑ ***You can gain 12 extra days per year just by clearing your desk. Put in a more negative way, that's 12 paid days wasted. Your boss will notice this.***
- ❑ ***MESSY DESKS COST MONEY!***

How to start clearing up the mess

> *❝ I got to work one Monday morning and I saw that my desk was just an ocean of samples, printouts, newletters and God knows what. Something inside me snapped. I grabbed some bin-bags and just swept it all away. It felt great until two days later when I realised I'd also swept away the only copy of a report I'd been putting together over the previous couple of weeks. ❞*
>
> **– Richard Selvey, paper buyer**

You can do something about your untidy desk, but first a word of caution. There are some tactics that you should **not** use. Two approaches in particular should be avoided at all costs.

1. The "nuke it all" strategy – obliterate everything in sight and hope that there was nothing important to lose.
2. The "I'll just devote an extra ten minutes a day to clearing it all" strategy – like most resolutions, this one is usually broken within a day or so (most people never find those extra minutes and quickly lose the piece of paper on which they've written their pledge).

So, if you feel the urge to give in to your pyromania, take a cold shower and think again. Also, unless you change your attitude to organisation drastically, your empty desk will soon fill up again. There's always more useless paperwork ready to fill that space. Indeed, for a disorganised person, the sight of empty desk space is just too tempting – "Quick, let's get it filled!"

One of the most common reasons for a cluttered desk is the overwhelming fear of throwing away something valuable. Who knows? Maybe that old envelope that's been sitting there since 1988 might have a vital piece of information in it. Does this sound like you?

Tackling your messy desk is all about organisation. It's about having a system for dealing with paperwork coming in so that it has somewhere to go – for instance, does it go to somebody else or into the waste bin? Always remember: *A desk is for paper in transit.*

ACT!

Analyse your flow of paperwork and identify where it could go to:

- ❑ ***In-trays, out-trays or pending-trays sitting on the desk.***
- ❑ ***A nearby filing cabinet.***
- ❑ ***The wastepaper basket.***
- ❑ ***Forget paper, store the information on computer.***
- ❑ ***A file (not a land-fill) in the desk drawer.***

To clear your desk, do you need to find or create storage space? Keeping your desk free of clutter means you are going to need other places to store the paper. An untidy desk can often be a sign that there is no filing system (or, at least, a very ineffective one).

Simple but effective filing systems

Do you have an effective filing system? If not, you should think about investing in one right away. They come in all shapes and sizes, from metal cabinets to ordinary drawer units that accommodate suspension files. If you're short of floor space but have plenty of shelves you could use box files to store your stuff.

> *" I now have a series of shelves above my desk and labelled box files for my samples, trade magazines and stock reports. My desk is reserved for the nitty-gritty order processing and urgent files are kept in the desk-drawer files. I haven't lost anything since I re-organised. "*
>
> **– Richard Selvey**

ACT!

Review your filing needs and the facilities you have at your disposal.

- ❑ ***What do you have?***
- ❑ ***Is it enough for your needs today?***
- ❑ ***Will it fill up and pose a problem in future?***
- ❑ ***Do you use it properly?***
- ❑ ***Could it be more effective?***
- ❑ ***What do you need to do to improve your filing system?***

Divide and rule – master your paperwork!

Once you have somewhere for your papers to go, the next stage is to have a system for sorting them out. Each item will put different pressures on you.

- ***Some call for immediate action (and mean it).***
- ***Some ask for immediate attention (but don't in all honesty expect it).***
- ***Others can happily be filed away until needed.***

What you need to do is sort through incoming paperwork as soon as it arrives and divide it up according to the relative importance of each component. This neatly organises your in-tray into a priority order and makes it far easier to know where to start if you're facing a terrifying array of things to do.

> *" I finally got the message about the importance of being well organised after I overlooked a final demand from a credit company. I'd sorted out the money to cover the arrears but the bill was buried and I missed the deadline – my equipment was repossessed as a result. "*
>
> **– Ged Armor, MD of an estate management company**

Make sure you have a system for grading your paperwork in terms of importance.

- ***Look through whatever arrives on your desk as soon as possible. Set aside a certain time for doing so if needs be.***
- ***Immediately bin or pass on anything you can.***
- ***Put what's left into piles which reflect the urgency of the content. For example:***
  1. ***Must do today***
  2. ***Must do this week***
  3. ***Can wait until next week***
  4. ***Can be done whenever I have the time.***

ACT!

Here are some methods for **not** dealing with paperwork efficiently. If you find yourself slipping into any of these bad habits, stop and remind yourself of how you should be treating what's in your in-tray.

- ***First come, first served – so no matter whether it's a court summons, a letter saying you've won the Lottery or an advertisement for Sock Garters, every letter waits its place in the queue.***
- ***Lucky dip or the gold-panning procedure – open the letters or read the files at random, hoping that you will stumble on the nuggets.***
- ***Personal foibles system – reading and dealing first with the letters you most like to receive such as, perhaps, personal mail or an interesting flier from the local theatre or equipment supplier. The corollary of this is that anything that looks as though it might contain bad news – a letter bearing the stamp of the taxman, anything in an official brown envelope, i.e. anything important – could stay at the bottom of the pile and then get overlooked.***

An effective filing system and a means of prioritising your papers will ensure that you can keep your desk free of clutter and ready to cope with the really important tasks in a timely manner. You'll also avoid missing anything important.

Don't get snowed under – delegate

Can you delegate the filing to someone more efficient? Sometimes you just have to face the fact that others may be much more organised than you.

> *"I discovered that our receptionist was an organisational genius. She now sorts my mail, organises my daily priorities and keeps all of the files in order. No more disastrous oversights for me, and I've got more time for my customers!"*
>
> **– Ged Armor**

Many people have highly trained secretaries and assistants and make criminally poor use of their talents. They could be amazingly helpful if given the authority to do the filing and organising. Delegating means trust. It requires clear guidance and instruction but it could save you both time and embarrassment. Think: Is there someone who works with you who could help you get and keep your desk tidy?

There's more about what and how to delegate in Chapter Three.

Ten commandments for sorting out your desk life

If you can organise your desk, the rest of your work should organise itself.

1. The first step is to acknowledge that an untidy desk sends out negative messages about your ability. It has a financial cost, too, in terms of time spent looking for buried documents.
2. Open every letter and file as soon as it comes in. Scan the name of the sender to help you assess its importance.
3. Sort your paperwork out initially into "must read" and "can throw away right now" categories. (The latter might apply to junk mail – unless you're a junk mail freak and, yes, there are some!) Throw away the throw-away-able NOW – don't let it get a taste for your desk, put it where it belongs.
4. If you know that some papers are important but you don't have time to read them now, put them in a special pending-tray. Set aside a part of the day when you *will* be able to read them.
5. Every morning, divide your incoming work into priority piles: (1) Must do today; (2) Must do this week; (3) Can leave for a week or more; (4) Can file this paper away now.
6. Establish a filing system that allows you to move the low priority work off your desk to a place where it won't be forgotten – hanging files in your desk drawers or a box file on a shelf above your desk. Create space for papers which can be archived.
7. Make an area on your desk for files or papers that fall in category (1) – arrange them in order of importance and start to work through them right away.
8. Once a job is done and you have finished with the paperwork, make a point of either filing it away in the right place or putting it in the bin.

9. Worship your waste-paper bin – throw into it as many sacrificial offerings as you can.

10. Look for ways of delegating the task of filing and managing your paperwork. There might be people in your department who would excel at the job and liberate more time for you to deal with the essentials. If you can organise your desk, the rest of your work should organise itself.

Ask yourself which of these ten commandments you should start working on now. The rewards are great – with an organised desk and an effective filing system your working life will be far more efficient and you'll always leave the office with a clear conscience.

Make Priorities, Meet Deadlines

Chapter 

What's in this chapter for you

Stop being a fire-fighter
Meet "impossible" deadlines
Prioritise
Profit from lists and planners
Exploit your diary
Tactics for prioritising and meeting deadlines

“ *I seem to be a slave to events at work. Any plans I may have for the day tend to get buried under new work and constant crises. I just never seem to be able to make any headway.* ”

– Gill Watson, accounts supervisor

> **Does Gill's problem sound familiar? Do you arrive at work with a clear plan of action only to find that, as soon as you start, piles of additional work suddenly appear?"**

Stop being a fire-fighter

Your life does not have to be a string of constant crises and impossible-to-achieve deadlines. If you spend most (or at least a good proportion) of your working day dealing with problems as soon as they arrive, you will inevitably find that you are getting behind on more important work.

"Fire-fighting" is destructive. If you continue to live and work by responding to every crisis immediately it arises you will become:

- ***stressed***
- ***disheartened***
- ***unable to plan strategically***
- ***exhausted.***

The key to beating this tendency is to avoid treating every task as top priority. You need to learn to take control of your time, set your own agendas and start to prioritise your work effectively. Let's analyse what is happening when another desperately urgent task comes your way.

You will probably recognise some of the following situations.

- ***The phone rings when you are in the middle of a vital report. A key customer is complaining that their last order has not arrived yet.***
- ***Your boss calls. He needs the month-end figures now, not for the end of the week as originally discussed.***
- ***An urgent memo from personnel arrives demanding a detailed reply by the close of business that day.***
- ***One of your colleagues walks in with a seemingly insurmountable problem and it takes you an hour to discuss it.***

Such scenarios occur because you are willing to jump to other people's deadlines and allow them to impose their priorities on you. You must learn to develop a method of establishing what needs your immediate attention and what can wait. You are not paid to try to please those around you all of the time!

You will learn more about how to prioritise your work later in this chapter. In the meantime, here are some introductory tips.

The first steps to help you avoid constant fire-fighting

- ***Identify the sources of crises. Is there a weakness in a particular department that means their problems always end up becoming yours?***
- ***Convince yourself that you should work according to your own priorities, not those of others.***
- ***Learn to say: "This problem must take its place in line – it's got to wait its turn." Practise saying it to yourself until it trips easily off the tongue.***
- ***Always explain to your tormentor the effect his or her demands are having on your other work. Establish in their mind and in yours that this is a serious problem.***

Meet "impossible" deadlines

"I seem to get memos on my desk virtually every day saying things like 'this is top priority' or 'please deal with this right away'."

– Gill Watson

Unless you are literally dealing with life or death situations, the word "urgent" is much overused. Generally it is employed by others to bully you into dropping all of your other work. Here are some reasons why you may be continually coming up against impossible deadlines.

- ***You always accept other people's deadlines unquestioningly.***
- ***You set unrealistic deadlines to please clients or colleagues.***
- ***You don't delegate tasks.***
- ***You aren't honest about problems encountered.***
- ***You never try to negotiate extended deadlines.***
- ***You don't differentiate between a phoney crisis and a real one.***
- ***You don't learn from your own mistakes.***
- ***You don't encourage others to learn from their mistakes.***

How can you avoid these mistakes or deal with deadlines which others are always giving to you?

You should start by realising that deadlines are always relative and are often open to negotiation and compromise. You should not always accept the first deadline suggested by a customer, client or your boss. It is always tempting to say "yes" to every deadline in order to appear willing, supportive and efficient, but by doing so you are very likely to annoy people or lose custom by missing the promised deadline.

Avoid "deadly deadlines"

- ***Check your diary carefully before accepting any deadline, however trivial. Remember, it's the trivial deadlines that mount up!***
- ***Check all the facts before you accept a deadline. What exactly is it that the person needs and in what form? Will a partly finished job, a précis maybe, suffice?***
- ***Be firm – if you know it can't be done in time say so and set your own deadline (a realistic one of course!).***
- ***Negotiate to arrive at a date which allows you the time to complete the task comfortably.***
- ***Break the job down into different stages and set mini-deadlines for each stage. This will ensure that you can keep to the final deadline.***

“These days I refuse to accept deadlines suggested by a client or colleague if I know that they are unrealistic. I use their deadlines as a starting point for negotiating more time.”

– Ray Cunningham, site supervisor

What if an agreed deadline turns out to be unachievable?

What do you do if you realise half way through a job that there is no way you can do it on time? The worst thing in such circumstances is to do nothing and hope that no one notices. Another common error is to imagine all sorts of impractical ways of finishing the job such as:

- *“I'll work all night on this.”*
- *“I'll give up my weekend to do it.”*

This is a slippery slope to a life of overwork, exhaustion and stress.

Here are some tips to help you get out of trouble if you have a deadline that you know you cannot meet.

TIPS

Hot deadline tips

- ***Calculate the risk of missing the deadline. What will the consequences be for you, your job or the organisation? If the risks in reality are low, miss the deadline but apologise as soon as you can to the person waiting for the work.***
- ***If you foresee a problem, try to extend the deadline as far in advance of the due date as possible. Be candid with the person waiting. People will respect you for being honest with them.***
- ***Ask for help – you might be able to farm out some of the work or share it with colleagues or friends.***

If you do miss the deadline, offer the person some kind of compensation. A small gift or a discount on the next order may help you to maintain some good will.

Prioritise

One of the major ways to start leading an organised life (as opposed to a chaotic and stressful one) is to learn the ability to prioritise. This will take a bit of practice but if you learn to do it successfully you will free up a lot of time and energy that would otherwise be spent worrying and panicking.

The first step towards being able to effectively prioritise your work is to realise that not everything needs to be treated as "equal top priority". Similarly, don't treat the latest thing that hits your desk as the most important.

It may be that you already have some kind of system in place. This might include one of the following:

- ***Doing things in strict time order – either the first job in is the first one out or conversely the last job in is the first job out.***
- ***The boss's requests are attended to first, the most junior person's last.***
- ***Gauging the relative importance of each request – the most urgent thing is done first.***
- ***A random system whereby you do a job if you are in the mood to do so***

Any of these systems can work if your workload is steady and predictable. However, all of them have a degree of inflexibility which means that it may prove difficult to accommodate a really urgent task.

One way to prioritise your tasks and still remain flexible is to create a three or four tier "jobs list" (a similar method is used in Chapter Four when we look at paperwork). These lists are divided by priority:

- ***Priority 1** is "important **and** urgent", i.e. drop everything and do it now.*
- ***Priority 2** is "urgent but not important" – perhaps you could delegate part of this task.*
- ***Priority 3** is "important but not urgent", it can be left a few days.*
- ***Priority 4** is "not important and not urgent" and you can do it whenever you have some free time.*

List all of the jobs which you handle and put them into the above categories. Here are some examples to help you.

- ❑ ***Priority 1** – the shop has run out of cash, the boss demands a report tomorrow morning or you suddenly learn that you have to step in and make a presentation to a major customer this afternoon.*
- ❑ ***Priority 2** – there is an agenda to prepare for next week's meeting, you have to see a major client the day after tomorrow or you have a long report to present at the end of the week.*
- ❑ ***Priority 3** – you have to book a time to take a major client out for dinner.*
- ❑ ***Priority 4** – you want to redesign the layout of the office or think about next season's catalogue.*

Be determined to use this system for all future work – it will give you an instant idea of where to start.

The only effective way to reduce your stress levels and become organised is to learn how to prioritise your work. You might also need to become more assertive with those around you in order to be fully in control.

Hot tips for dealing with your priorities

- ❑ *Once you have categorised your work into priorities 1, 2, 3, and 4, think about the best time of day to tackle each. Perhaps the last hour of each day, when you may be winding down, is the best time to deal with those less important category 4 tasks.*
- ❑ *Put all the jobs within each category into some kind of order. For example, if you have six priority 2 tasks to do, three of which you do not enjoy, start with one of the unpleasant jobs and reward yourself by tackling a less onerous task next. Continue by punctuating the dull with the interesting.*
- ❑ *Schedule all of these tasks in your diary – never do a job unless it is there (see below).*
- ❑ *When a new task comes in, prioritise it as above, order it within that category and make a diary note of when you are going to do it.*
- ❑ *Try wherever possible to do priority 4 jobs quickly. Do not let them eat up important time.*

Profit from lists and planners

We have already touched on the use of lists above but their importance cannot be overstressed. Try to keep a pen and note pad with you always (even beside your bed!) and use it to feed your "to do" list. You can then split this into your priority groups – this activity should always be done before you leave the office so that you have clearly defined objectives for the next day.

> ❝ *I've got a huge planner on my wall. All of my jobs are scheduled on it and I use a colour coding system to show the priorities. It's really handy when people come in and try to pile more jobs on me – it shows them graphically what I've already got to clear. They see for themselves what is and isn't possible.* ❞
>
> **– John Dolan, production manager**

It's true, wallplanners are another useful aid to getting organised. They are cheap to buy or can be made quickly. They will show you at a glance an entire year divided by days and months. Key jobs can be marked in, showing the start dates and when they should finish. You can also block out entire days on it when you are scheduling to tackle a major task.

Make sure that it is positioned so that you can always see it when at your desk. By using this you can see at a glance when important deadlines are looming. It also speaks volumes to other people who are trying to add to your workload.

Exploit your diary

> ❝ *I used to pride myself on always being able to keep everything in my head – deadlines, appointments, things to do. This system worked for the first few months in my new job but I then started to miss important meetings and appointments. It became blindingly obvious that I could not rely on my memory alone when in one week I managed to miss an important meeting with my director* **and** *was two hours late for a key customer. I now don't move without consulting my diary.* ❞
>
> **– Cath Robbins, key accounts manager**

A diary is not just for appointments. It should also be used to schedule when you need to start particular jobs and what the completion deadline is. For example, with priority 1 tasks, you can use your diary to break down each job into stages. An example might look like this:

March 9th: Start collecting information for April sales presentation
March 12th: Check hall is booked and refreshments arranged
March 21st: Sort information received
March 22nd: Meet designer to discuss graphics
March 31st: Finished slides needed
April 1st: Prepare hand-outs
April 3rd: Finish first draft of presentation
April 7th: Amended draft
April 14th: Final draft
April 18th: Rehearse to colleagues
April 21st: Presentation to sales team

Your diary should be with you always and if used properly will prove a key tool in being organised. And remember, don't just keep it to yourself. If you have a personal assistant or secretary, update them on your plans weekly and ensure that they are aware of your schedule. That way, if work comes in for you in your absence you need not be committed to it.

Tactics for prioritising and meeting deadlines

Organising your workload better is the key to getting things done on time.

TIPS

Use prioritisation effectively

1. **Get out of the habit of fire-fighting by questioning the importance of tasks which are landed on you at short notice. Make it clear to other people what responsibilities you already have and get into the habit of saying "it'll have to wait its turn".**
2. **Learn to set and stick to your own priorities. If you are forced to take on further tasks, find out exactly what's involved and work out your own deadline rather than accepting one that's handed to you. Say: "That deadline isn't feasible – it will take at least until . . ."**

3. Divide all of your jobs immediately into priority categories: 1 – vital, do now; 2 – urgent, do today, delegate the parts you can; 3 – important, but there is some time to spare; 4 – routine tasks which you can do at your leisure.
4. Use the likely consequences of missing the deadlines as a further means of prioritising very urgent work. Negotiate flexible deadlines where possible and be forthright in admitting to slippages.
5. Compile a categorised "to do" list for the next day before you leave work in the evening. It should give you a place to start as soon as you arrive next morning.
6. Record all of your start dates and deadlines in a diary or on a wallplanner so you can see at a glance what's looming. This will ensure you don't forget anything and also help you explain to others why you cannot take on their work too.

By getting your priorities right, you will take control of your work life and meet your deadlines. If everything is going to plan – and it's your plan – you will feel pride in your efficiency and extreme stress will be a thing of the past!

DELEGATE WITH CONFIDENCE — Chapter 3

What's in this chapter for you

Delegate – or sink
What is delegation?
How to recognise what to delegate
Selling delegation to those around you
How much to delegate
Knowing who to delegate to
What's cramping your delegation style?
Tips for delegating effectively

> ❝ *It always seemed to be me who was snowed under with work. I was permanently stressed out. What made it worse was that the rest of the team and my so-called support staff seemed not to have a care in the world. The office to them was just a place to chat to their friends while I was gradually sinking under hundreds of 'urgent' priorities.* ❞
>
> **– Rita Norman, design consultant**

Does Rita's experience sound familiar? Most people experience overwork – the 'too much to do, too little time to do it' syndrome – but find it very difficult to delegate any of it.

Delegate – or sink

Reluctance to ask others to take on work is very common, especially among new managers.

Do you feel under constant pressure at work and yet can't delegate some of the tasks to others? Could this be because:

- ❑ ***You feel they lack the knowledge or are not reliable enough to tackle the work?***
- ❑ ***Your boss has asked you to do the job so the buck stops with you?***
- ❑ ***You are frightened to ask – others, particularly your boss, might think you are not up to the job?***

You should always remember that this is not just your problem, it affects everybody in your workplace. Overwork and the stress that this leads to is a serious problem not just for individuals but also for their employers and their colleagues. Stress-related illness is one of the major causes of absenteeism and puts additional pressures on the entire structure of the organisation.

> “ *I’ve just had a month off due to what my doctor described as a minor nervous breakdown. Since the restructuring at work two years ago, things just piled up on me. I wasn’t sleeping properly because of worry. I was staying late at the office and working most weekends. All of this was putting immense strain on my family life. What I realise now is that a lot of the pressure could have been relieved if only I had delegated more of the routine tasks. I didn’t, partly through fear that in the next restructuring I would be seen as replaceable and partly because I didn’t trust those around me to do the job properly.* ”
>
> **– Bob Clough, warehouse manager**

The causes of Bob’s health problems are fairly typical – poor organisation, the inability to delegate and fear of being seen as unable to do the job you’re paid for.

What is delegation?

To organise yourself effectively, you need to understand what delegation is. Let’s start with some examples of what delegation does not mean.

Delegation is not:

- ***Being able to shirk your responsibilities***
- ***Dumping work you don’t like doing on others***
- ***Tricking people into doing your work.***

In other words, delegation is about sharing your responsibilities, not shirking them. It means empowering others by trusting them to help you.

Do you need to delegate? Look at the list below. If two or more of the statements apply to you, the chances are that you need to learn to delegate more effectively.

Symptoms of the need to delegate

- ***"I always feel under pressure through overwork."***
- ***"I have to work stupidly long hours just to keep in touch."***
- ***"I am always taking work home with me at the end of the day or at weekends."***
- ***"My staff are always coming to me with problems that I feel they should be able to deal with themselves."***
- ***"When I do delegate, it is always with the nagging fear that it will not get done as well as if I were to do it myself."***
- ***"I end up spending an inordinate amount of time checking and correcting work that I have delegated to others."***

To delegate effectively, you must learn to do so for the right reasons and with confidence. Like many skills in business, it is more of an art form than a science and is not something that you can pick up overnight. You need to learn from experience (and experiment), but by getting it right you can reap an enormous reward.

The first person you need to convince about the importance of delegation is **you**. Think carefully about your current predicament and the problems that poor delegation causes you. If you still feel hesitant about getting on with it, remind yourself of the very real benefits delegation can offer.

Delegate effectively and you will:

- ***At last find the time to get on with what is really important to you and to your business***
- ***Feel far more in control***
- ***Avoid constantly having to waste time fire-fighting***
- ***Motivate and empower those around you, thereby improving everybody's work life.***

How to recognise what to delegate

❝ I'd love to delegate more to my staff but I can always find excuses not to. I feel guilty about being seen to be dumping work on others – they are all up to their eyes in work themselves and I do not want to add to their problems. Also, I can never get organised enough to work out the right tasks to give them! ❞

– May Davids, office manager

It is ironic that busy people are often so immersed in their work that they cannot find the time to analyse their daily workload and plan how to save time by involving others. The work just keeps piling up and everyone else seems so busy that there is never an opportunity to work out who should being doing what. In the end, rather than thinking long term, many of us take the easier option of simply getting on with everything ourselves. This is a very common trap to fall into – and it is very difficult to get out of.

The first step to resolving the problem is to analyse carefully the time you are spending at work. You can do this outside of work hours if necessary.

- ❑ ***List all of the tasks that you have spent time on over the last week. Make it as comprehensive as possible.***
- ❑ ***Divide the list into tasks which took under 15 minutes, between 16 and 30 minutes, and longer that 30 minutes.***
- ❑ ***For each item on the list, ask yourself: "Did I HAVE to do that job?" If you answer "no", write down the name of someone else at work who could or would be able to have done that job.***

Your list of tasks might look something like this:

Less than 15 minutes

Making tea/coffee in the morning
Opening the post
Listening to answerphone/voice-mail messages
Answering the telephone

16- to 30-minute tasks

Sorting out work rotas
Filing
Chasing invoices
Unscheduled meetings with staff

Tasks taking more than 30 minutes

Attending meetings
Composing letters
Writing up minutes of meetings
Compiling reports

Now write down against each task the name of someone else who could have done it instead of you, given the right training and support.

Finally, work out a plan of action for delegating similar generic tasks in the future.

Here is an example of what your completed list might look like for the tasks taking less than 15 minutes.

Task	*Who else could do it?*	*Action plan*
Making morning coffee	Alan or Kerry	Ask them tomorrow
Opening the mail	Jane	Arrange a meeting to explain your sorting method
Listening to messages	Kerry	Ask her to make daily lists
Answering the telephone	Alan or Jane	Divert your calls to them first and brief them as to what should be transferred to you

Get the picture? Already, by addressing yourself to the smaller tasks, you are freeing a sizeable amount of your time without piling a huge amount of work on to those around you.

" I decided to work out precisely where I was becoming bogged down at work. I commute by train and I spent the journey on two consecutive days analysing all the tasks I had undertaken in the past week. I was amazed by how many of the jobs I was doing on automatic pilot and which should and could have been done by others. "

– Carol Seers, surveyor

TIPS

Tips for starting to delegate effectively:

- ❑ *Invest time in looking at how you spend a typical week.*
- ❑ *Recognise those tasks that you can delegate and those that you need to do yourself.*
- ❑ *Assign some of those tasks to others.*
- ❑ *Be aware of how you present these new duties to those around you – more on this later.*

Selling delegation to those around you

" I decided to delegate all my more boring and repetitive tasks to my two assistants. I worked out who should do what and sent them a memo setting out their new responsibilities. I was understandably worried about their ability to do the jobs to my standards so I asked them to report their progress to me on a daily basis. The result of this exercise was that two perfectly charming and co-operative assistants became embittered and irritated and seemed to resent my every instruction. One left last month, the other has just handed in his notice. So much for the powers of delegation! "

– Nigel Casey, MD of a printing company

Nigel's experience is an object lesson in how not to delegate to staff. Once you have assessed your average daily workload and recognised the kind of tasks which take up your time fruitlessly, you need to sell the idea of delegation to those around you sensitively and positively.

Delegation should offer some perceived advantage to both parties. Nigel committed the following cardinal sins:

- ***Only passing over the mundane tasks***
- ***Delegating via memo***
- ***Not having the courtesy to discuss or explain the new tasks face to face***
- ***Not being seen to trust his staff with even the dull jobs.***

In Nigel's case we have learnt how not to do it. To successfully delegate you need to know about the strengths and weaknesses of those around you and then discuss with them the positive benefits of taking on the new work.

Make a list of those people who report to you and their strengths and weaknesses. Now, try to link each member with given tasks that you want to offload. For example:

Task	*Talent needed*	*Person for the job*
Reorganise database and keep it up to date	Computer skills and problem solving	Kerry
Answering incoming calls	Good telephone manner and selling skills	Paul
Modify filing system	Organisational skills and attention to detail	James

ACT!

Certain work might require a whole range of personal qualities. If that is the case, apply the same methodology but break down the job into smaller tasks and then allocate people to each of these.

When you have decided what tasks you are going to delegate, you must ensure that you consult properly with your staff. They may feel nervous about the new responsibilities which you are giving to them – they may feel resentful about taking them on. You need to build up the positive aspects.

Try the following tactics to sell your idea:

- ❑ ***"I know how good you are at organising systems. I'd like to use your expertise in helping to . . ."***
- ❑ ***"I know how ambitious you are. By taking on this role it will really help you with your career development."***
- ❑ ***"You have been doing so well recently that I want to involve you more in how the department operates."***

But remember, transparent flattery will not endear you to your staff. It would be difficult, for example, to sell the positive career benefits of washing up the coffee cups every day, so only use these approaches if you *sincerely* believe in them.

So, you have talked your new plans through with your staff. Listen to their responses. If they feel daunted by new responsibilities then you need to offer support. This can be by way of extra training or staying involved in the task yourself for the first few weeks.

Tips for selling delegation

- ❑ ***Allocate tasks in a way that plays to the strengths of those around you.***
- ❑ ***Present the delegated tasks as a challenge.***
- ❑ ***Use delegation as a means of showing trust.***
- ❑ ***Discuss new roles face to face with your staff.***
- ❑ ***Offer support and training if necessary.***

How much to delegate

Delegation is not an absolute. There are degrees of delegation ranging from delegating nothing and expecting in return no initiative at all to devolving full responsibility for all your workload to others. In between these two extremes lies a range of options, such as:

- ❍ ***Ensuring your staff only act according to your precise instructions***
- ❍ ***Allowing degrees of discretion and initiative – but they must check with you first***

- ❍ *Recommending courses of action but leaving the choice to those people involved*
- ❍ *Letting them get on with the job as they see fit but ensuring that they report back each result to you*
- ❍ *Allowing your staff to decide how to do a given task and letting them get on it with, reporting back to you on a routine basis only.*

To delegate does not mean to give up all involvement. Different degrees of delegation fit different circumstances. For example, you may bring your staff in and consult with them fully on a course of action before making the final decision yourself. You may wish to set up a team to take on a new project and, even though you are on the team, everybody has an equal voice and decisions are made collectively.

Knowing who to delegate to

Choosing the level of delegation is one way to help you decide who to delegate to. But remember, it all comes down to trusting and respecting your subordinates. Be prepared to offer assistance freely to someone who has the right characteristics but, perhaps, not enough experience.

You have a responsibility to train your delegates. As they learn, you can step back and even extend the level of delegation.

Tips on who to delegate to

- ❑ *Audit your staff's talents to identify potential candidates for the responsibilities you want to pass on.*
- ❑ *Choose the person whose skills most closely match the requirements of the job.*
- ❑ *Ask yourself how much of a challenge the new task will pose to that person. Will they rise to it?*
- ❑ *Decide what level of delegation you wish to offer. This will depend in the early stages on the experience of the delegate.*
- ❑ *Make it plain you are there to give support – mentoring, regular meetings, whatever is needed. With the right person and the right guidance, you could kiss goodbye to the whole job.*

“When I really thought about the tasks I was doing each day, it became clear that the other members of the team could benefit and learn from being given some of them . For example, I always used to take the first briefing meeting with a new client, a process that could take days and involve being out of the office for long periods. It dawned on me that Mary, a fairly junior member of staff, had most of the qualities needed to do the job well: an excellent listener, attends well to detail, able to summarise ideas well and very personable. With a couple of days' training, she was ready and willing to face the clients on her own. She is now doing an excellent job, the clients like and trust her and she is growing daily in her professional abilities and destined for great things. I now have time to stay on top of the more strategic aspects of my job.”

– Jill Gutteridge, owner of a textile manufacturer

What's cramping your delegation style?

You have learnt in this chapter the importance of effective delegation and how to pass on the right tasks to the right people. But you should also be aware of many of the common reasons why people stick to their old ways and insist on taking on everything themselves.

The commonest reasons for not delegating are:

- **Guilt** – *"I'm paid to do this, not my staff."*
- **Worry** – *"What if they mess it up – how will it reflect on me?"*
- **Insecurity** – *"Will I be seen to be superfluous?"*
- **Dislike of change** – *"It's always been like that here, who am I to change it?"*
- **Fear of losing status** – *"Will I be seen to be less effective?"*

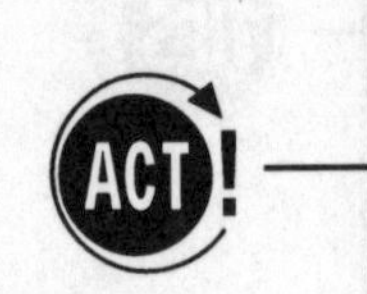

If you feel any of these fears flaring up, snuff them out by reminding yourself that not everything is your problem alone. Experiment with simple tasks and build on your successes. If you want to organise your life in the way you want, delegation is an essential skill.

- ❑ *Your team will help if you are asking for help rather than dumping on them.*
- ❑ *Delegating will make the work flow through easier – no boss will view this negatively.*

- ❑ *Mistakes can soon be eradicated if you brief well and follow up with support.*
- ❑ *Imagine how much more effective you could be if you liberated more time to devote to your top-priority work!*

Tips for delegating effectively

Don't waste time doing things that others could do instead

1. Work out why parts of your job need to be delegated and sell the idea to the most important person – YOU.
2. Set aside time to make a full audit of the tasks that you regularly undertake.
3. List those tasks which could be delegated to others easily – and those which could be delegated with more training and preparation.
4. Look at the skills of those around you and wherever possible match the tasks to their abilities.
5. Present new roles in a positive manner – stress the personal gains that will accrue to the delegate and your trust in their ability to carry out these tasks.
6. Don't dump just the mundane tasks on others – hand over interesting and developmental work as well.
7. Provide those you delegate to with support, encouragement and resources.
8. Make clear how little or often you expect your delegates to report back to you. Keep a watchful eye in the early stages so you can steer them in the direction of success.
9. Once a task has been successfully delegated, relax – don't interfere . . . LET GO!

If you follow these basic rules then you will soon master the difficult but vital art of effective delegation.

PROCRASTINATION, PAPER AND PHONES — Chapter 4

What's in this chapter for you

Stop procrastinating
Tackle your paperwork
Keep your in-tray empty
Make the phone your friend
Master your paperwork and the phone, now

“*I just don't seem to have the ability to do things well or on time. It takes me ages to get started on certain tasks and the result is that I am at least three weeks behind where I should be. I thought I was covering my tracks well, but just recently one of our key suppliers put our account on hold because I hadn't unpacked their last delivery and so their invoice hadn't been sent to accounts. I have just received a written warning from my boss.*”
– Anil Patel, warehouse manager

Do you seem unable to do make a start on really difficult tasks? Are there times when you just cannot face particular kinds of work? Do you find yourself making excuses for not beginning something? Does the thought of cleaning out the coffee machine seem more attractive than beginning the report to the MD?

Stop procrastinating

Most people suffer from a tendency to procrastinate in some form or other. The effect is that you will end up behind on your work, and other jobs will come in pushing the first task further down the pile of unfinished business. For some, the thought of a looming deadline, a livid boss or an angry customer is the only thing that will spur them to get a job started.

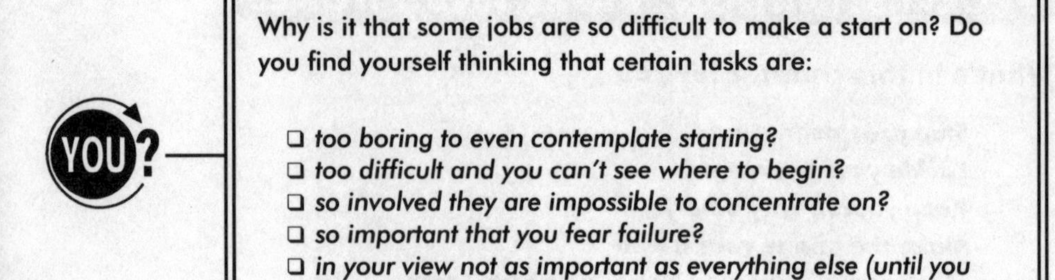

Why is it that some jobs are so difficult to make a start on? Do you find yourself thinking that certain tasks are:

- ❑ ***too boring to even contemplate starting?***
- ❑ ***too difficult and you can't see where to begin?***
- ❑ ***so involved they are impossible to concentrate on?***
- ❑ ***so important that you fear failure?***
- ❑ ***in your view not as important as everything else (until you find out otherwise when the boss shouts at you).***

Instead of getting on with such tasks, it is all too easy to find ways of avoiding doing them, such as:

- ❍ ***thinking of other jobs you would rather do;***
- ❍ ***sharpening your pencils, making coffee, watering your plants (i.e. displacement activities);***
- ❍ ***phoning a colleague, ostensibly to share vital information but in reality for a good gossip.***

Procrastination, putting things off until tomorrow, is the enemy of good organisation. It will cause you to be inefficient and could result in severe difficulties at work, as in the case of Anil. This chapter will help you to overcome the dangerous tendency to procrastinate.

Getting started

The first stage in dealing with procrastination is to understand what is stopping you from getting started.

Let's look at those possible reasons for delay in more detail.

1. The job is too boring

- ❍ ***Split the task into manageable chunks.***
- ❍ ***Reward yourself when you finish sections – allow yourself that chatty phone call, a sociable cup of coffee or even ten minutes reading the newspaper!***
- ❍ ***Plan regular but strictly controlled breaks.***
- ❍ ***Add in little bits of interesting work – for example, if you are writing a report, include projects of particular interest to you.***

2. The job is too difficult

- ❍ *Ask for guidance or extra training.*
- ❍ *Speak to your manager, explain your problem and ask for more time.*

3. You can't concentrate

- ❍ *Break the task down into smaller sections and set time limits for finishing each one.*
- ❍ *Ensure you finish each section before your attention wanders.*

4. The task is so important that you fear failure

- ❍ *Work out a worse-case scenario – what will happen if you do fail? If potential disaster awaits, then use the pressure to motivate yourself. If the task is not really that important then put it into perspective – life will go on and you will have learnt from your mistakes.*
- ❍ *Anticipate possible criticism – prepare your boss or client by saying that you are finding the job difficult and it may not be perfect.*
- ❍ *Share your fear with your boss, a colleague or a friend – you'll probably find that they'll help you to realise that the fear of failure is entirely unfounded.*
- ❍ *Analyse your goals – are they too difficult to achieve? If your standards are ridiculously high then you'll be so worried about achieving them that you will find it difficult to get started.*

5. This task is not as important as others

- ❍ *Put ALL of your tasks on to your priority list (see Chapter Two).*
- ❍ *Recognise that you have to start somewhere to clear the backlog.*
- ❍ *Reward yourself when you have cleared something from the list.*

The key to overcoming procrastination is to get started somewhere. Looking at mounds of work and worrying about them will get you absolutely nowhere.

By setting realisable goals, and rewarding yourself for your achievements, you can make inroads. Similarly, by setting priorities (and checking that the priorities of others conform with your own) you will find that the tendency to procrastinate can be controlled.

> *"My workload was getting ridiculous. Everything was top priority and I was spending all of my time looking at my heaving intray and worrying. I solved the problem in two ways: first, I worked out the true priorities of the work I was receiving from my boss and then I shut my office door and just got started. I now feel much more in control."*
>
> **– Debbie Cooper, management trainee**

Tackle your paperwork

> *"Paperwork seems to be self-replicating. Every day the pile on my desk just gets bigger and I find myself ignoring it until such time that I cannot see over it. I then simply bundle it all up and put it in any empty space I can find. I figure that if something is important then it will be brought to my attention by someone at a later stage."*
>
> **– David Beckett, recruitment consultant**

Does David's problem and solution seem familiar? Despite claims that the paperless office will soon be with us, most organisations seem still to generate masses of the stuff. You need to work out effective methods for dealing with your paperwork or you'll sink beneath it.

Think about the paper in your life:

- ❑ ***Do you have a constant stream of new paperwork arriving on your desk daily?***
- ❑ ***Do you never find the time to split it into things that need your attention and things that should go in the bin?***
- ❑ ***Are you frightened of being ruthless and throwing things away just in case they prove useful in the future?***
- ❑ ***Would you like to work out a system for handling the paper, but don't know where to begin?***

You need to be determined to make a start on tackling paperwork now. It **can** be done and the beneficial effects will mean that you never again feel snowed under.

How to tackle the paperwork mountain

- *Set aside part of each day (even if it is only fifteen minutes) for dealing with paperwork. If necessary, schedule this in your diary and be obsessive about using that time effectively.*
- *Create a holding bay for material such as journals and routine memos that you may or could need at some future point. An alphabetical concertina file is very useful for this. Every three months, discipline yourself to clear this file out.*
- *Avoid the "paper carousel" system, where the same piece of paper keeps appearing in front of you. Once you have read a document, mark it for action, file it or bin it.*
- *Commit yourself to dealing with at least one terminally troublesome piece of paperwork a day. But, don't deal with too many unpleasant jobs at once – spread the pain!*
- *Establish a ritual whereby every month you have a "blitz day". Get bin liners, sacks or boxes and fill them up with accumulated junk.*
- *Think green! Speak to the local paper recyclers and ask them to come in every couple of weeks to collect. This will encourage you and others in your company to be ruthless in throwing away unimportant paperwork.*

Keep your in-tray empty

> " *I use my in-tray for all mail that comes to me daily. The result is that it keeps building up with the stuff I can't clear by the end of the day. I can never find anything quickly and I can never prioritise my work.* "
>
> **– Colin Hartley, distribution manager**

There is nothing more likely to stop you getting organised than an over-full and disorganised in-tray. As we saw in Chapter One, your in-tray should **not** be used a general storage area.

If your in-tray is full, look at the reasons and the remedies:

- *You have no system for prioritising paperwork – then use the four-level hierarchy we introduced in Chapter One and split it up.*

- ❑ ***If you are using it as a "temporary" storage area, don't** – make separate storage areas for all but the highest priority documents.*
- ❑ ***You can't bring yourself to dump junk mail** – if you must keep it, create a separate tray . . . watching it grow out of control should persuade you to be more ruthless.*

Once you've convinced yourself that paperwork is something you must subjugate and you have overcome your procrastination, the secret is simple. Simply start to prioritise every piece of paper as you receive it and find an appropriate places to put them – **not** your in-tray unless that item is a top priority document.

It should be child's play but there are psychological hurdles to clear before you can prioritise what goes into your in-tray. Be aware of these pitfalls so you can sidestep them.

- ❍ ***It's a fax or an e-mail – it must be urgent! (NO! No matter how high-tech the message, it's the content you need to assess. Look at each of them coldly and file them in the place which reflects their priority level – you can get junk mail by fax and e-mail as well as through the post.)***
- ❍ ***Your boss has given you the deadline! (Relax, think about it. Bosses always want everything yesterday – if you're hard pressed already, go and talk to your boss to explain what priorities you already have and establish where his or her "request" fits in.)***
- ❍ ***You have promised a favourite colleague or customer that it will be done by a given time! (Don't avoid telling people that you can't meet their deadline if it conflicts with other agreements – you may lose lucrative new business.)***

The important thing here is to be open and devolve the decision about priorities if you foresee an in-tray conflict. For instance, if company policy insists that certain kinds of letters are replied to immediately (e.g. a letter of complaint from a customer) but you still have a backlog from yesterday, then make the point to your superiors. There are only so many hours in the day.

Tips on tackling your in-tray crisis

- ❍ *Handle each piece of paper once and once only. Either work on it immediately, file it to be worked on at a scheduled time in the future or bin it.*
- ❑ *If it helps, create a "what am I supposed to do with this?" file to collect documents you don't know how to categorise. However, you will need to pare it down on a regular basis.*
- ❑ *If reports or memos of no concern to you keep hitting your desk, find out who is sending them and ask them to stop.*
- ❑ *Practise techniques for assessing what is genuinely urgent and important, and therefore worthy of a place in your in-tray.*

Make the phone your friend

❝ It seems that as soon as I find a spare hour to really get on top of my work, the telephone rings and my schedule goes to pieces. I find it very difficult to keep conversations with certain people short and sweet. ❞

– Stefan Elgy, area sales manager

Having a telephone can be a mixed blessing. Where would we be without it? And yet, it can be an unwelcome and intrusive presence in any office. When it rings, there is always the pressure to act immediately, to the detriment of your other work.

How often do you encounter these problem with the phone?

- ❑ *Calls are wrongly diverted to your department.*
- ❑ *Callers demand that you deal with their queries immediately.*
- ❑ *You can't seem to keep the call short and to the point.*
- ❑ *It always rings when you are in the middle of a task that demands total concentration.*

You need to learn how to use the telephone as an aid, not a hindrance. The above problems and many other similar ones can cause enormous disruption unless you control the impact of phone calls on your work life.

Cut out the negative aspects of telephone communications

- *Install an answerphone or voice-mail service. When you don't want to be disturbed, divert your phone accordingly.*
- *Try to encourage callers to fax you the details of what they are asking. This will focus their thoughts, encourage brevity and give you a permanent record which is more difficult to overlook than hastily scribbled notes.*
- *Set a time limit on calls made or received, and stick to it. Start off by saying you are busy and you will have to go in five minutes.*
- *If you really do not have time for the call, say so. Be polite but firm and fix a time when you can call back.*
- *Make sure your diary and note pad are to hand when you take a call so you can take down details and discuss appointments or schedules without being railroaded.*
- *Where possible, appoint a "gatekeeper" – someone to take calls on your behalf. You can then decide in what order to deal with calls or, indeed, if they can be delegated.*

On the question of telephones, a word for home-based workers everywhere. If you have an office in your house, then ensure that you have a separate business line with an answerphone service. Nothing is more soul-destroying than being at the beck and call of customers and clients all day (and all night if you are dealing overseas). Never give out your private number to business colleagues and switch off the bell on your phone outside office hours.

Master your paperwork and the phone, now!

To improve your work life, you must learn to deal effectively with the two of the biggest time wasters at work – uncontrolled paperwork and phone calls. And you must do it **now**.

Don't be enslaved by mountains of paper and endless phone calls

1. Acknowledge the time you lose if you're overwhelmed with paperwork which you have no means of dealing with. Resolve to do something about it right away.

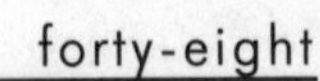

2. Start to prioritise your workload immediately and establish a "storage" system which gives you places to file work from every category – important jobs in your in-tray, non-important documents elsewhere.
3. Make a point of dealing with at least one task you dread every day and don't bury things in a "guilt heap". Make sure also that you aren't looking at documents more than once – action them, file them or bin them!
4. To motivate yourself to get straight down to work, break down long tasks into manageable chunks and reward yourself for completing difficult jobs.
5. Set aside a fixed time each day for dealing with your in-tray. And make it a habit to regularly sort through the less important "pending" space you have created – throw out as much as possible, especially junk mail and other "might be useful in future" paperwork.
6. Encourage everybody to have clear-outs by instigating regular visits from your local paper recycling company.
7. Protect yourself from telephone interruptions with an answerphone or voice-mail. If possible, use someone else to filter your calls.
8. Set time limits on your calls and make them clear to yourself and the caller by stating what they are at the beginning of the conversation.
9. Prioritise your phone calls in the same way as you would your paperwork and "to do" list.

Following the guidelines given in this chapter should set you well on your way to becoming more organised and efficient in the office.

MAKE THE MOST OF MEETINGS

What's in this chapter for you

Meetings under the microscope
How to cut out wasteful meetings
How to evade meetings
Minimise the pain
All-important preparation
Take control
Making meetings effective

Take a look at your diary. How many meetings did you attend over the past six months or so? Some research suggests that business meetings take up on average two days of a working week. Few companies seem able to survive without meetings and the trend appears to be on the increase.

> *" My organisation seems to work on the principle that 'when in doubt, hold a meeting'. I wouldn't mind if they were productive but, frankly, most of them are a waste of my time and just increase my backlog of work. "*
>
> **– Terry Ford, production director**

Meetings under the microscope

It is true to say that most people find meetings at work frustrating and unproductive. However, with a bit of clever organisation, you can make sure that that you get the information you need without wasting time unnecessarily.

The way to start is to analyse carefully what happens in the meetings you attend.

Think about the last meeting you attended

- ❑ *What was the purpose of it?*
- ❑ *Did it achieve that purpose?*
- ❑ *How vital was it that you attended?*
- ❑ *How could it have been improved?*

Bad meetings = bad business

By wasting staff time, a badly run or superfluous meeting will cost a business money. Here are some common symptoms of a badly organised or ill-conceived meeting.

- ***It went on too long.***
- ***One or two people hijacked the agenda for their own purposes.***
- ***Too much time was spent on trivia.***
- ***It turned into a brain-storming session when it should have dealt with the key issues.***
- ***There was no proper agenda.***
- ***You did not get the chance to put your point of view across.***
- ***It took several hours to get to the meeting and the bit relevant to you lasted for just ten minutes.***
- ***It was just an opportunity for the boss to lay down the law.***

You can add your own experiences to this list. The point is that once you can recognise a bad meeting, you must act to turn it into a good one or find ways of not having to attend.

If, like in Terry's business, your company seems to hold meetings just for their own sake, you need to reduce your suffering to a minimum. There are tactics you can learn which will help you achieve this.

How to cut out wasteful meetings

If you run meetings, or at least have a say in how they are conducted, you should be aware of the costs of running them badly.

> *“I calculated that our firm spent around 20 hours a week in meetings. That involved six managers at about £30 per hour – that's £180 per hour. With secretarial and other incremental costs counted, our meetings were costing upwards of £4000 each week. I circulated these figures to my colleagues – mysteriously, our meetings are now much shorter and less frequent!”*
>
> **– Simon Bradley, personnel manager**

Putting a money value on the meetings in your company is an effective way of making people take stock of the worth of them.

Make sure that everyone knows the true costs of every week's (or month's) meetings. Send round a memo, or put it on the agenda of the next meeting and get it minuted.

How to evade meetings

Meetings should give everybody a chance to have their say. If that is not happening in your case then you should be questioning why you attend. If all you are getting out of going is some information, then ask to be excluded and simply read the minutes.

> *" If I get invited to attend a meeting that I suspect is going to be a waste of time, I ask the person how I can contribute. It very often makes them think about who they are inviting. "*
>
> **– Jane Freedman, marketing manager**

There are some useful tactics to help you if you want to avoid attending a meeting or wish to have it cancelled or postponed.

Evasion tips

- ❑ ***Suggest holding a smaller scale meeting, with only those people who can really contribute in attendance.***
- ❑ ***Try this: "Couldn't we discuss this informally in your office?"***
- ❑ ***Always ask to see the agenda in advance. If it seems irrelevant to you, suggest that the meeting could be postponed or turned into a less formal gathering.***
- ❑ ***Delegate someone else to go in your place.***

Minimise the pain

Assuming that you have tried the above tactics and they have failed – you have to attend – with some forward planning you can ensure that the costs in terms of time or boredom are minimised. Here are some key tips on how to do this.

- *Read the agenda carefully beforehand and ask that those parts which are relevant to you are dealt with first. Ask to leave once these items have been covered.*
- *Insist that the meeting is kept to a tight schedule. Even if people are late, it should start and finish on time and each item on the agenda should have a precise slot allocated to it. If it overruns, then ask for it to be guillotined.*
- *Speak to the chairperson beforehand about the need to squash irrelevant speeches and waffling.*

It can also be effective at the end of the meeting, when the "dates for the next meeting" are discussed, to ask "do we really need one?" and remind everyone of the cost implications.

All-important preparation

The best meetings are those that are well planned. Start with the agenda, which should always be circulated in advance to all those attending. Study it carefully and make notes on the issues of concern to you. Now you are ready to get to work.

Pre-meeting preparatory work

- *Lobby people for their support beforehand on those issues of most importance to you. By doing this, the meeting may just become a speedy formality.*
- *Identify and isolate anyone you know has conflicting views to yours and who may cause difficulties. Either try to get them on your side beforehand or ensure that you have enough support in order to successfully argue your case.*
- *If there is a daunting length of time set aside for the meeting, prepare those around for the fact that you will have to leave before it finishes. If your input is valued, then this will encourage everyone to speed up!*

If you are regularly expected to attend meetings and are frustrated by having to do so, you need to stop being passive. With good preparation and awareness of the clock, you can start to make things happen your way.

Take control

> *I became so sick and tired of useless meetings that I decided to take control of how they were being organised. I knew I had to gain influence to make sure that everbody's time was not being wasted.*
>
> **– Mandy Sims, store manager**

If your meetings aren't getting better, accept that you'll have to be more assertive. The first step is to stress the positive – what should successful meetings achieve? They should:

- ***motivate the people in attendance and help team building;***
- ***produce a positive outcome for everybody present;***
- ***make everyone feel involved and part of decision-making processes;***
- ***help tangibly to increase profits and reduce costs.***

> *The meetings were being badly chaired so I circulated a memo which clearly stated the problems. Everyone seemed to agree with me and a few days later, I was voted in as chair. It wasn't an ambition of mine but I'm glad I took it on – our meetings are now short and useful.*
>
> **– Mandy Sims**

If you are successful in taking control of a meeting, there are some core practices you should begin to implement immediately.

Managing meetings

- ***Circulate an agenda well in advance.***
- ***Make sure that the meeting is held at a time and in a place that is convenient for everybody.***
- ***Set clear rules and guidelines for behaviour – everyone getting there on time and respecting the opinions of others.***
- ***Give less assertive colleagues the chance to be heard.***
- ***Insist on sticking to the agenda, thereby politely stopping people with a tendency to waffle.***
- ***Ensure that the meeting and all items on the agenda run to time – finishing early would be even better!***
- ***Circulate minutes as soon after the meeeting as is possible, with clear indications for follow-up action.***

Finally, remember that once you have gained control of a meeting don't lose it! Be determined to run things properly and effectively – remind yourself of the cost implications of doing otherwise!

Making meetings effective

Meetings can squander a lot of your precious time and certainly make it harder for you to get yourself organised. The solution is to make them work for you rather than against you.

Master your meetings

1. **Work out and circulate the costs involved in holding meetings. This can focus other people's attention on getting more value from them.**
2. **Never go to meetings unprepared. Work in advance on the agenda issues which are important to you so your case is more persuasive.**
3. **Try to doctor the agenda beforehand so that the points relevant to you are covered first. You can then work out a way of leaving early!**
4. **Ask why you have been invited if you are at all doubtful about the benefits of attending.**
5. **If possible send someone else instead, using the positive delegation skills we learnt earlier.**
6. **Insist that all sections of the meeting run to time. If anything overruns, ask for it to be cut.**
7. **Use the "dates of the next meeting" discussion to argue for not having one.**
8. **Lobby for support beforehand and try to get possible trouble-makers on your side.**
9. **If you need to, hijack the chair – run the meeting yourself!**

With planning, thought and organisation, wasted hours spent at boring meetings while your important work is piling up can be a thing of the past!

Making Computers Work For You — Chapter 6

What's in this chapter for you

What your computer can do for you
Managing your information
Office suites – the all-in-one solution
Organising your life the electronic way
The paperless office
Get the most from computers

> " *When our firm computerised my heart sank. I was afraid of my computer but, by asking my colleagues to help me, I finally got the hang of it. Now it makes my life so much easier that I can't imagine how I coped before.* "
>
> **– Pam Flew, accounts administrator**

It's often too easy to forget that if you strip away all the high-tech jargon (and there's plenty), modern computers are designed to make your life **easier**. The electronic wizard in the box is clever enough to write your letters, file away your paperwork, or find documents that would otherwise be buried under an avalanche of paper. They can even schedule your days and work out how to organise the most complex of projects.

Is the computer in your office (you do have one don't you?) your slave or master? Do you know what it can do? Do you squeeze out every benefit it can offer?

What your computer can do for you

There isn't room in this book to go into all the benefits of modern computers. Suffice to say that they have become staggeringly clever and so much easier to use in the last few years. The software is now very straightforward. On-screen instructions lead you by the hand (or fingers) to do the right thing. So, if you used to be afraid of computers, take a look at the latest models.

What can a computer (and its software) do to help make your life more organised? This chapter describes some of the things to look out for. Let's assume that you are working with a PC (which is what most people have unless it's an Apple Mac). Let's also assume that it has enough power to run popular business software.

Wordprocessing

You can buy wordprocessing software to help you write and store documents. You can create any number of documents (letters, faxes, memos, reports, even books) and store them clearly in directories that are easily found – no more trips to the filing cabinet. If you forget the name of the document, most software will even find it for you if you give it a key word to search for.

Have you always felt: "I'll never understand this wordprocessing stuff?" If so, despair no more. The latest wordprocessors have incredible on-screen tutors that actually show you how things are done.

Using "macros" you can, for instance, create standard reply letters. One press of a key and the whole letter appears on screen. You can easily customise the letter with any name or address kept in a list. Documents can be then printed out, saved or faxed directly from the PC. The latest software will show you how to create a macro in a matter of minutes.

Other time-saving features of wordprocessing software include: grammar and spelling checkers (some will even correct for you as you write); a series of automatic document layouts to choose from; simple "desk-top publishing" facilities that allow you to create newsletters, fliers, brochures and so on.

If you are intimidated by the software, invest in some one-to-one computer training. No matter what people say, most computer literature is written by the techno-literate for the techno-literate. Also it can take weeks to wade through happy, smiley guide books and tutorials. A day with an expert showing you how to work the machine and its software will save you weeks of bitter frustration.

Can't be bothered to type? If you are a slow typist or don't have the time, modern computers can save you the effort. These days you can scan a page of text directly into your computer so that it instantly appears on screen as a file that can be saved, amended or printed out. You can even get special software that allows you to dictate directly to your computer – it translates your speech into words on screen.

Managing your information

When it comes to sorting out your "information" a computer is the ideal tool.

> *" I carry all my client information in a database on my laptop computer. It's like having your own portable filing cabinets and I am now never without all the details I need. "*
>
> **– Mary McGuire, sales manager**

Databases

Mary uses a piece of software known as a "database". A database can store vast amounts of information in any form you want. Think of it as a very clever electronic card index that can arrange information into names, addresses, towns, areas of interest and so on. A database can be used to print out mailing lists, or instantly find information on customers, rivals or colleagues.

> *" We update all our customer information just by typing in the data under the appropriate heading. Then if I want to find all the customers, for example, that live in Scotland, or all those who spent more than £3500 in the last year, one press of a key and all the information suddenly appears. This can be printed out or presented as a colour chart or a graph. It's great and so easy to use. "*
>
> **– Mary McGuire**

Spreadsheets

Want to calculate projected profits (or losses) for the next three years? Or write a business plan? Spreadsheet software is all you need. This allows you to enter numbers, dates, words or formulae on to a grid of rows and columns. In this way the computer can keep track of your cashflow position, projected profit margins, business projections, statistical analysis and so on. Although it may take you a little time to set up your spreadsheet, once there it is very easy to use and you can print out results as charts, graphs and other forms of fancy eye-catching graphics.

Other information management software that you will find useful includes:

- ***Accounting packages, some of which produce reports which may be acceptable to your tax authorities. This software does all the hard work of an accountant without the annual fees.***
- ***Personal finance money managers which keep track of your current financial position (if you really want to know!). They also keep a record of your bills and regular outgoings.***
- ***Payroll software which calculates your payments to staff, including wages/salaries, overtime, bonuses and so on.***

Office suites – the all-in-one solution

Before investing in expensive software, look at the many excellent packages that call themselves "office suites". These are bundles of software that perform several tasks: wordprocessing, database, spreadsheet, calculator, business presentations, personal information manager and so on. These all-in-one packages usually contain pretty powerful software that can handle most of your needs as an individual or small business. There's also the extra advantage that each function can be integrated with the others. As an example, you can call the information on your spreadsheet into your wordprocessor so that your next letter or company newsletter contains the latest company accounts, cash projections, sales targets and the like.

TIPS

Tips on buying

- *Ask for a demonstration of how the software works before buying. You may also be able to try it out on a free trial basis.*
- *Ask for software that has an "on line tutor". This will show you how to use the product.*

- *Make sure that the software comes with telephone support. You should be able to call a number and ask for help and advice if you get stuck. The software support person can talk you through the problem. (I once had to ask how to switch the machine on!)*

Organising your life the electronic way

> “*I bought one of those little electronic organisers last year, and wouldn't be without it now. I input all my useful phone numbers, dates, addresses. I can jot down reminder notes and even get the thing to give me an alarm call when a meeting is due. How I ever lived without it I'll never know.*”
>
> **– Brian Mitchell, local authority manager**

Are you forever fiddling with bulky personal organisers, diaries and notebooks? If so, you could throw them all away and invest in a small, compact electronic organiser.

Organisers

The best organisers are highly versatile mini-computers that have a variety of functions:

- ***wordprocessor** – with the appropriate software you can transfer the documents you write on to your PC (and in some cases, vice versa);*
- ***database** – where you can keep all your personal and customer information;*
- ***spreadsheet** – this offers the facilities we saw above and allows you to experiment with figures by asking "what if?" questions;*
- ***an address book and telephone list** – with some models you can even dial the number direct by holding your telephone over the organiser;*
- ***calculator;***
- ***current time at home and around the world;***
- ***the facility to e-mail or fax messages to anywhere in the world and receive replies;***
- ***a daily appointments diary or "things to do" list which can often be viewed by the day, week, month or year.***

On some organisers, you can enter a diary date and have it automatically repeated for regular meetings and events. The appointments diary can also be programmed to block in your meetings and give you a warning when you try to double book yourself.

Watch out for the cheap organisers which do not operate as a computer. They are useful, but very limited things that can merely record names, addresses and numbers.

Laptop computers

If you've got the cash, consider buying a laptop computer. These are fully fledged, book-size computers with proper keyboards, colour screens – everything you would expect on a desktop PC. Laptops are much more expensive than PCs but they offer the advantage of being able to be used wherever you are – on a train, in the car, in someone else's office and so on.

Laptops are powered either by battery or mains electricity. You can install sound cards, CD ROMs, fax cards and extra memory. By saving information on disk you can transfer it between your laptop and your office computer.

There are some potential drawbacks to laptops. Watch out for these:

- ***some of the cheaper ones are not very well made and don't like being moved around, which defeats the object;***
- ***good ones are very expensive;***
- ***some of the screens are difficult to read;***
- ***the batteries don't last very long.***

Despite what the sales person tells you, or what it says on the box, most laptops will only run for an hour or so on full use. Either you take extra batteries (expensive) or use the computer very sparingly. Plug it into the mains if you can.

The paperless office

> *" My laptop computer now has one of those modem gizmos – this means that I can attach it to a telephone point and send faxes and e-mail. For somebody who's on the road as much as I am it's great because it's like having your office with you. "*
>
> **– Chris Riley, hotel inspector**

A modem is a small attachment fitted inside (or sometimes outside) your computer. This lets you connect the computer (or electronic organiser) to the outside world via a telephone point. You'll need special software to set it up but this usually comes with the modem. You can then, for instance, type up a document in your wordprocessor and, instead of printing it on paper, fax it to someone else direct from your computer to a remote fax machine or another computer fitted with a modem and the appropriate software.

A modem also gives you the opportunity to communicate via e-mail This is another way of transmitting documents electronically but this time via the Internet. The advantage of e-mail is that you can "download" large documents in seconds. At the other end, the person receiving your e-mail can work on the document to finish it and then send it back to you – no paper or postal delay!

E-mail is a great way for people who are a large distance apart to work together. To use e-mail you will need:

- *a computer fitted with a modem – the faster the better (a "28.8" should be adequate);*
- *an account with an Internet provider, who will usually allocate you with an address (although you can choose your own e-name) and charge you a modest monthly subscription;*
- *the e-mail addresses of the people you want to communicate with.*

Get the most from computers

If you have the right equipment and software, and you know how to use it properly, your productivity will be enhanced beyond your wildest dreams.

Getting the right system for you

1. If buying a desktop PC beware of warranties that say "back to base". Imagine shipping a bulky computer back to its factory or service HQ hundreds of miles away. Repairing them can also take a long time. Ask the computer company to lend you a PC if yours needs repairing.
2. Ask for "on site" service which means that the engineer comes to you if anything goes wrong.

3. Try to get the maximum warranty on your laptop. Some companies offer two years' parts and labour. They are very expensive to repair so make sure you have some kind of service guarantee.
4. When choosing software, make sure you have a clear idea of what you want it to do and ask for a demo to check it's up to the job.
5. Invest in some one-to-one training. This will save you hours of frustration trying to fathom what language your manual is written in!
6. Talk to someone who uses an organiser. See whether it could revolutionise your life. If you decide to buy, watch out for cheap ones which don't offer the full range of facilities.
7. Look at "office suites". These offer you a complete package of wordprocessing, database and spreadsheet software.
8. Get a modem and plug yourself into the telephone lines. Once you have one, you'll be able to transmit faxes and documents direct from your computer and you can begin to enjoy the time savings and simplicity of e-mail.

Once you have overcome any technophobia and seen how user-friendly modern computers have become, you will never look back. Now you really can Get Yourself Organised!